MONKEYS OF CENTRAL AND SOUTH AMERICA

A TRUE BOOK

by

Patricia A. Fink Martin

Children's Press®

A Division of Grolier Publishing

New York London Hong Kong Sydney
Danbury, Connecticut

The emperor tamarin has a long mustache.

Reading Consultant
Linda Cornwell
*Coordinator of School Quality
and Professional Improvement
Indiana State Teachers Association*

Content Consultant
Kathy Carlstead, Ph.D.
*National Zoological Park
Washington, D.C.*

The photograph on the cover shows a golden lion tamarin. The photograph on the title page shows a three white-faced capuchins.

Visit Children's Press® on the Internet at:
http://publishing.grolier.com

Library of Congress Cataloging-in-Publication Data

Martin, Patricia A. Fink, 1955–
    Monkeys of Central and South America / by Patricia A. Fink Martin.
        p. cm. — (A true book)
    Includes bibliographical references and index.
    Summary: Describes the physical characteristics, habitats, life cycles, and behavior of New World monkeys, which live in South and Central America.
    ISBN: 0-516-21574-4 (lib. bdg.)   0-516-27017-6 (pbk.)
    1. Cebidae—Juvenile literature. [1.Monkeys.] I. Title. II. Series.
QL737.P925M37   2000
599.8'5'098—dc21
                                                              99-17063
                                                              CIP
                                                              AC

Contents

Do you like to climb trees?

What Is a Monkey?

Can you imagine what it would be like to live in a tree? You could spend your day running along branches and swinging through the treetops. Most people have trouble just climbing trees. Swinging from branch to branch seems almost impossible.

It is not impossible for monkeys. They do it all day long. Monkeys are perfectly adapted for living in trees. Most monkeys live in the world's rain forests.

Monkeys are a type of mammal. Scientists place them in a group of mammals called primates. Chimpanzees, orangutans, and humans are primates too.

Primates are smart, curious animals. They have eyes in

The chimpanzee (left) and the orangutan (right) are both primates.

the front of their heads, so they know whether the objects they see are nearby or far away.

Monkeys can use their hands and feet to grab branches, peel fruit, and shell nuts.

The hands of primates are different from those of other mammals. Primates have slender fingers and a thumb, so they can pick up and hold objects.

This black howler monkey can use its prehensile tail to hang from a tree.

Some monkeys can also grab things with their prehensile tail. A prehensile tail can bend at the tip. It acts like an extra hand. Some monkeys use their tail to hang onto branches. The end of the tail can wrap around a branch.

Monkeys Are Like Us

There is a patch of bare skin at the tip of a monkey's tail. This skin acts like our fingertips. It's used to touch and feel things. It also has tiny ridges that give the tail a better grip.

You have tiny ridges in your skin too. To see them, you'll need a pencil, a sheet of white paper, and clear tape. Use the pencil to darken a small area on the paper. Then rub a fingertip across the pencil marks. Now stick a piece of tape on your finger. Peel off the tape, then put it on the white paper. Do you see the swirls and circles?

This boy is making a copy of his fingerprint.

This squirrel monkey uses its tail to balance while it takes a quick drink.

Two Kinds of Monkeys

Monkeys with prehensile tails belong to a special group of monkeys called New World monkeys. These animals live only in Central and South America. They are different from the monkeys of Africa and Asia.

This squirrel monkey lives in a national park in Colombia.

All American monkeys live in trees. They have wide noses. Some have claws on their fingers instead of nails. They also have lots of teeth— thirty-six in all! Do you know how many teeth you have? Count them.

These monkeys are called New World monkeys. Many years ago, explorers from Europe sailed across the Atlantic Ocean and discovered North, Central, and South America. Because these lands

In the late 1400s and the 1500s, explorers such as Christopher Columbus visited the Americas. They called this land the New World.

were new to them, the sailors called them the New World. They called the lands they already knew about (Europe, Asia, and Africa) the Old World.

Of course, every part of the world is really the same age. Most people do not use these terms anymore. But scientists still name the two groups of monkeys in this way—New World monkeys and Old World monkeys.

The Pygmy Marmoset and the Cotton-top Tamarin

A brown furry creature pops its head out of a hole in a tree. Soon other furry heads appear. In a flash, the furry family dashes up the tree trunk. Then the quick little

Pygmy marmosets are furry little monkeys.

animals disappear among the leafy branches.

These animals are pygmy marmosets—the world's smallest monkeys. They are so tiny that one could easily sit in the palm of your hand. Marmosets live in small groups called troops. They are as active as squirrels.

A pygmy marmoset is small enough to fit in the palm of your hand.

They spend most of the day feeding. They eat small insects, spiders, and fruits. Marmosets also bite little holes in trees and lap up the sap that oozes out.

Have you ever tried tree sap? You have if you have eaten pancakes with maple syrup. Maple syrup is made from the sap of maple trees. Pygmy marmosets drink the sap of trees that grow in South America.

This cotton-top tamarin has quite a head of hair.

Cotton-top tamarins are pretty little monkeys that live in the South American country of Colombia. They get their name from their fancy hairdo. A fountain of long, white hair flows from the top of their head.

Tamarins live in small family groups. Each group is led by a male and female pair. Each year the female has twins. Both parents take care of the babies. When the young tamarins are hungry, their mother feeds them milk.

When the family moves from place to place, the father carries the twins on his back. He also plays with the

A young cotton-top tamarin stays close to its parents.

babies and picks insects and dirt out of their fur.

Tamarins are a lot like pygmy marmosets. They are small and sometimes feed on tree sap. From head to rump, tamarins are just 8 inches (20 centimeters) long. Even though they are small, tamarins can make plenty of noise. They tweet and twitter as they move through the trees looking for food. They like to eat fruits and insects.

A Parade of Monkeys

Woolly monkeys live in the rain forests of South America. They like to climb high in the treetops. If these monkeys fall, they save themselves by grabbing a branch with their tail.

Woolly monkeys live in groups. They roam the forest

This woolly monkey uses its tail to grab tree branches.

together, looking for food. They eat mostly fruits. At midday, the adults rest. They pick insects and dirt from their thick, soft fur.

During the hottest part of the day, woolly monkeys rest in the trees.

These monkeys are usually very friendly. They rarely fight, and they often greet one another by kissing!

Howler monkeys are found throughout Central and South America. When a howler monkey roars, the sound can be heard for miles. It sounds like the horn of a freight train.

This monkey has a special structure in its throat. By pushing air through it, the howler can make quite a racket.

This howler
monkey lives
in a rain forest
in Belize.

Howler monkeys eat fruits and leaves.

Howlers are large, slow-moving monkeys. They spend half of the day resting. They often hang by their tail while feeding on leaves and fruits. Even at rest, their tail curls tightly around a branch.

The spider monkey does not have eight legs. But when it hangs upside down with its hands, feet, and tail wrapped

Does this monkey remind you of a spider?

This spider monkey lives in Costa Rica.

around a branch, this monkey looks a lot like a spider.

These monkeys live in large groups. During the day when they search for food, they usually break up into smaller groups of two or three. Their favorite foods are ripened fruits. At night, the large group comes back together.

Night monkeys live in forests from Panama to Argentina. Unlike other monkeys, night monkeys sleep

Night monkeys wake up at dusk and begin to search for food.

A night monkey's big eyes help it see in the dark.

during the day and hunt at night. They like to eat fruits, but they also catch insects.

Night monkeys can see in the dark with their owl-like eyes. On very dark nights, these monkeys quietly search for food. But when the moon is bright, they are more active. They hoot loudly for mates and may fight with one another.

This woolly spider monkey lives in the rain forests of Brazil.

Monkeys in Danger

The rain forests of Central and South America are very special places. Where else in the world can you see a monkey that hangs by its tail? Or a monkey small enough to fit inside a teacup? Or a monkey that feeds like a vampire on tree sap!

Sadly, some of these monkeys are endangered species. The cotton-top tamarin is one of them. Its relative, the golden-headed lion tamarin, may be the rarest monkey in the world. Only a few hundred are left in the wild. Woolly monkeys, spider monkeys, and howlers are in trouble too.

Many New World monkeys are hunted for their meat and their fur. Some are sold

Only a few golden-headed lion tamarins are left on Earth.

As rain forests are cut down or burned, monkeys lose their homes.

as pets. Monkeys that manage to avoid hunters have another problem. Their homes are being destroyed as people clear land for wood and for farming.

What will happen to these night monkeys if their forest is destroyed?

These red howler monkeys are a lot like us. Do you think we should try to save them?

The forests of Central and South America are disappearing fast. If the places where monkeys live are destroyed, they will not be able to survive. The forests give monkeys shelter and food—everything they need to live.

Would you like to help the monkeys? Tell others what you've learned. Join a club. Work with others. Help save and protect these amazing animals.

To Find Out More

Here's a list of additional resources. Use them to learn more about these monkeys and their forest home.

 **Books**

Harman, Amanda. **South American Monkeys.** Benchmark Books, 1996.

Lessem, Don. **Inside the Amazing Amazon.** Crown Publishers, Inc., 1995.

Maynard, Thane. **Primates: Apes, Monkeys, and Prosimians.** Franklin Watts, 1994.

Patton, Don, **New World Monkeys.** Child's World, 1996.

Rinard, Julie, and National Geographic Staff. **National Geographic's Amazing Monkeys.** National Geographic, 1994.

Organizations and Online Sites

The Golden Lion Tamarin Management Committee
National Zoological Park
Department of Zoological Resources
3000 Connecticut Avenue, NW
Washington, DC 20008

International Primate Protection League
P.O. Box 766
Summerville, SC 29484
http://www.ippl.org

Mad About Marmosets!
http://loki.ur.utk.edu/ut2kids/primates/marmosets.html

Read an interview with Dr. Suzette Tardif, an assistant professor of anthropology at the University of Tennessee, Knoxville. Dr. Tardif has been studying marmosets and tamarins for most of her adult life.

The Nature Conservancy
Adopt-an-Acre Program
1815 North Lynn Street
Arlington, VA 22209

Rainforest Action Network
221 Pine Street, Suite 500
San Francisco, CA 94104
http://www.ran.org/kids_action/index.html

World Wildlife Fund
1250 24th Street, NW
Washington, DC 20037
http://www.wwf.org/

Important Words

endangered species living things that are in danger of dying out

mammal an animal that has a backbone and fur, is warm-blooded, and produces milk for its young

prehensile a part of an animal that can grab or grasp things

primate a mammal with eyes in the front of its head, hands that grasp, and a large brain

sap a sugary liquid found inside plants

Index

(**Boldface** page numbers
indicate illustrations.)

Meet the Author

Patricia A. Fink Martin has a doctorate in biology. After working in the laboratory and teaching for 10 years, she began writing science books for children. *Booklist* chose her first book, *Animals that Walk on Water*, as one of the ten best animal books for children in 1998. Dr. Martin lives in Tennessee with her husband, Jerry, and their daughter, Leslie.